"Hephzibah"

A collection of poems and prose
by Anna Hands (aged 8-18)
inspired by Ecclesiastes 3 vs 1-8

Published 2014 by arima publishing

www.arimapublishing.com

ISBN 978 1 84549 634 0

Printed and bound in the United Kingdom

Typeset in Palatino

Swirl is an imprint of arima publishing.

arima publishing

ASK House, Northgate Avenue
Bury St Edmunds, Suffolk IP32 6BB
t: (+44) 01284 700321
www.arimapublishing.com

"Hephzibah"

A collection of poems and prose by Anna Hands
inspired by Ecclesiastes 3 vs 1-8

∞

∞

∞

Hephzibah – 'my delight is in her'

Patience is...
a deep breath
the time before a storm
a calm anger
a cup quivering on the edge.
Patience is my mother.

There is a time for everything

And a season for every activity under the heavens

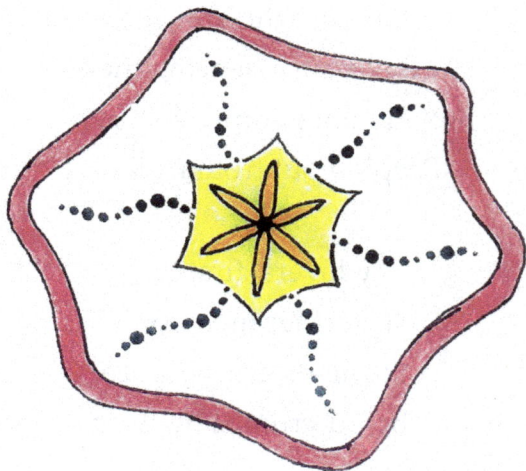

Whispers of the Trees

Standing sentinel,
Erect
In a world full of curves.
Guarding secrets as treasures,
Catching them like birds.
Stare into the branches
At the shapes dancing there,
You may glimpse a story
Peeping out from its lair.

Shy lovers' first kiss
Or murder most foul.
A toddler's grazed knee;
Betrayal in bread-crumbs by the pocketful.

Paper Dragons Per Annum

Cottage-cheese clouds and seas of grass,
Mountains of snowdrops and hills of glass.
Molehills and dewdrops sing in the rain,
Welcome the fairies of Spring again.

Jellied air on heavy days;
Graceless ghouls shimmy in heat haze,
Smouldering jowls of paper dragons,
Broiled grass shrivelling under flame.

Crunching golden browns, crisp leaves;
Scouring brush of a brusque breeze.
Imps flick conkers from lantern branches;
Twirling squirrels, nature's dancers.

Sparks of frost bounce and burn,
Rivers of ice twist and turn.
Wicked Witch of Winter Snow
In plains of perfect, pure show.

Come and Gone

Buds escape their wooden hiding places,
As golden trumpets from coffins of green
Burst forth, resurrected. All only to
Crumple in a frosty fist, crying tears
Of ice. Delicate petals unfurl, tentative,
In fragile sunlight. But that very light
To which they entrust their safety and life
Is smashed by pebbles of steely water
And boulders of cloud as they tremble bruised
And battered. The flowers weep – the wolf howls
And the wind screams – Lightening taunts thunder who
Lunges down then splits the clouds with a crash.
The seas writhe in pain and churn in anguish:
The world cries at Spring come and gone so quickly.

Icy Warm

Inexorably round,
The path of sunlight;
Sinks over the horizon for
Half a span.

On the other side,
An eternity of cold
Steals the heat
Thick fur can't hold.

So burrowing down,
The powdered ground –
A fortress of icy walls
Surround.

Blocking out the dying light;
Premature shadows clothe the cold,
Turning to velvet warmth
As body heat unfolds.

Frozen darkness swirls above me,
But it is icy warm here in my cave.
Smooth wet walls of ice surround the
Drifts of dreams and sleep I crave.

Long months of slumber
End in hollow hunger.
A crack of light urging onward,
From the icy warmth of my cave.

A Garden Escapade

Green; all the same homely green. Though, through the shadow reflection of my face on the window, the raspberries wink from beneath vegetation and blackberries mock me with their sharp thorns. The smooth white plastic bowl clutched in my hands should be incongruous in these dewy surroundings but it fits perfectly with the gentle slope of nature. The grass has just been cut, stinging my nostrils with sharp scent. Tiger grass dots the ground where my feet plough through the wet clippings. A bird is singing somewhere; it seems silly that this sweet tinkling should be called a tune but it lifts my heart nonetheless. I pick the fruit absent-minded and yet totally focused, ignoring the thorns reaching for me. Studded pink and black jewels tumble, falling wetly into the white plastic. I duck to peer between green tendrils for that ruby glimmer of fruit. Intent, almost tense, the berries hold their breath in their leafy hiding places as my probing fingers creep ever closer.

But they are never discovered. An indignant twitter; I look up to find myself staring into the beady black eyes of my red-breasted host. He hops and flaps, keeping me under close surveillance. Not wanting to offend, I freeze, wishing him to remain. He deigns to charm me with his company for mere seconds before departing, with a final chirp.

The peace returning, I go back to the hidden fruit, my heart full and a small smile gilding my face. The stained white plastic looks out at the beauty of nature in envy, the green reflected in the eyes and heart of it. But it can partake in Mother Nature's hand: gathering berries, juices staining.

Golden fingers are releasing their grip, colour draining like a drawn out sigh. In the gradual darkness, a wet, earthy smell thrusts itself into recognition and the quiet rustlings of... of? Secret things emerge into the darkness, following the light, taking their turn to control the tranquillity of this place. The secret things which chase you from their solitude as you hurry back to light and warmth. You are only temporary; the endless tides of light and dark are forever.

Shooting Stars

We lie on our backs
Feeling the damp grass
Through the aged threadbare sheet
As the summer cold permeates us
And the dark gradually reveals
The wonders of a cloudless night.

We lie swaddled in blankets,
Staring upwards
As celestial objects
Trace delicate paths
Above us.

We lie chattering loudly
As if to fill the immense
Space between us
And those pin pricks of light
Scattered across the heavens –
Powder paint sprinkled across the sky.

We lie wondering how
Those stars swimming above us could be
Burning boiling smouldering
Balls of gas
Larger huger brighter
Than we could ever imagine
And so far away.

Surely, it can't be but a lie!

A time to be born and a time to die,
A time to plant and a time to uproot,
A time to kill and a time to heal,
A time to tear down and a time to build

Driftwood

We all start out
Cut from a tree
And then:

Dropped off the back of a hulking lorry
From a cliff top road
Into The Sea –
A loose tie-down

Or from that house
That home
Which was taken by
The voracious hunger
Of the salty waters

Or else wind and rain
Battered and buffeted
A ship – a storm
Cracked it like an egg –
'Til it sank down and down...

But be you from hull or head-board,
Poop-deck or door-frame,
You are in the same Sea now,
To be chipped and smoothed by the same waters.
The waters determine how
And on what soft sands
Or hard pebbles
Or sharp shingle
You'll wash up.

Of course,
Some will get stormy weather,
Vicious undercurrents to skyscraper breakers,
And some may get calm
Gentle reflections of the blue sky and soft sun,
But all will get worn,
Quick or slow.

Sure, it makes a difference
Whether you're hardwood
Or plywood.
Plywood'll be smashed soon.
Hardwood is stronger stuff,
Made of stronger stuff.

Time may change
But we all go the same way
In the end,
Be we Loon, Buffoon or Tycoon.

Ever-Changing

Currents of minerals form, flow,
Or don't flow, and break down again
In the eternal process of change in which
A mighty tree can grow from the speck of a seed.

We are just witnesses during our lives,
Spirit and matter pushed together;
Only in death do we join this cycle,
And the two can return to their separate origins.

Our physical bodies go from oneness to the whole
Maggots feeding our essence back,
As our souls soar free of physical binds,
Free to be with and in the Holy One.

Lawn

A platform of clipped colour,
Subdued emerald;
Perfect before time has touched you.

But you sneak;
Past each second you scamper,
Stretching past the care I dealt.

Only time could nurture,
Nurture the growth of freedom;
Wild radiance of life expanding,
Until?
Again.

The Spider under the Cup

There is a spider
Under that cup.
It's been there for two days
But I can't pick it up.
What if it lives and is angry with me?
It could run up my leg if I set it free.
Or scuttle away under my bed
And remain in my dreams as a phantom instead.

There is a spider
Under that cup.
It's been there for two days
But I can't pick it up.
What if it's dead and covered in mould?
If that were true, it would all be my fault.
That poor little spider died sad and alone.
Would I like to die in a cup on my own?

Inferior Creation

A 3D criss-cross of dappled green
And wrinkled brown
Spreads up around me.
Anomalies flit through empty spaces,
An inexplicable part of this pattern,
Though separate.

I too am an anomaly, am separate,
As I walk between the spaces,
Adding my footsteps
To the thousands of eroded feet
Which stretched a tiny ribbon
Into a highway.

From these strips of ownership
We view and claim this pattern,
In the pretence that we could control it.
So far superior to our own textbook creations,
This Organised Chaos
Can be nothing more than a complex aspiration;
Inspiration.

Shut up, Mr Smith!

You with the hat, and the dog, and the flat;
That squat, dull grey box of a flat. You with
Your well-tended gardens, front and back.
You paid for it, did you? Well, fancy that!
You seem a bit riled, a little upset.
It means that much to you? Now, now. Don't fret.
Odious man! It's just repossession.
Get off my back and shut up, Mr Smith!

"Don't be that guy." – Listen to your wife.
Of course we eavesdrop at windows! We care
For your life – insignificant and small.
No one will listen. No one at all. We
Are wise and know best for you – the voices
Of society do nothing without
Due democratic propriety. Don't
Argue or question. Shut up, Mr Smith!

You know Ms Doreen, at number fifteen?
She once was your neighbour but we drove a
Wedge in between, a JCB, so now
She is just 'her down the street'. You see, we
Flattened her house and built a new one there.
Perfect, she told us, but for the view. For
Your home is ugly, it devalues hers.
It's for her we say: 'Shut up, Mr Smith!'

A corp'rate machine? Stop making a scene!
Did you not hear what we did for Doreen?
Individual needs are top of our list
So t'is best to be quiet. You get the gist.
What really makes me titter is that you
Think you stand a chance in this legal dance.
We've a team of lawyers and you're alone,
So give it up and shut up, Mr Smith!

A time to weep and a time to laugh,
A time to mourn and a time to dance,
A time to scatter stones and a time to gather them up,
A time to embrace and a time to refrain from embracing

Graduation: A Right of Passage

At a time when the world is pushing forward,
A moment to reflect on times gone by.
Not with regret but happy sadness;
Joyful sorrow in long cloaks and mortar boards.
Fidgeting through speeches, it flashes by.
Throwing them in the air; a shower of successful lives.
Action marking the passage of the young
From past trials and tribulations and on to…
On to…?
On to the rest of their lives; individual lives,
Individual hopes, individual dreams.
Individual people.
Together for one last time.

High as a Kite

My strings are twisted and slack
And my ribbon lies in a tangle.
I drag my heels through the grass
Bumping and tripping along the way.

Oh for a breeze to lift my spirits,
Just a friendly gust to inspire flight,
A hand up as I climb
The azure rungs of the sky.

One blustery day, I'll soar high,
Fluttering my ribbon
And tugging at my strings,
Flirting with the wind.

Despite the little effort it takes,
Once there I can dart and wheel,
Laughing as I tie the clouds
Into knots of sunshine.

(It's a long way down.)

Old Photograph

The contours on your face
Mapped on this glossy page.
They seem so out of place;
These lines, these signs of age.

Those last few years, I felt,
Not beheld, your expression,
The way you talked, smiled, smelt.
You made a full impression.

I sensed your mirth as sunshine
But the sun has set too soon.
Now I make those crow's-feet mine
And wet this pale reflected moon.

Wishful Dreaming

I can feel your true heart beating,
The rise and fall of your chest,
The warmth of your breath in my hair
As I drift between two states of rest.

But your heart is a bag of mere eiderdown;
It's an open window which gives my hair lift;
Your warmth is my own, radiated back:
It is between dreaming and waking I drift.

Cuddles

Dad's don't equal Mum's,
Mum's can't equal sister's.
But cuddles from there,
are exceptionally rare.
So,
expect more from a teddy bear!

A time to search and a time to give up,
A time to keep and a time to throw away,
A time to tear and a time to mend

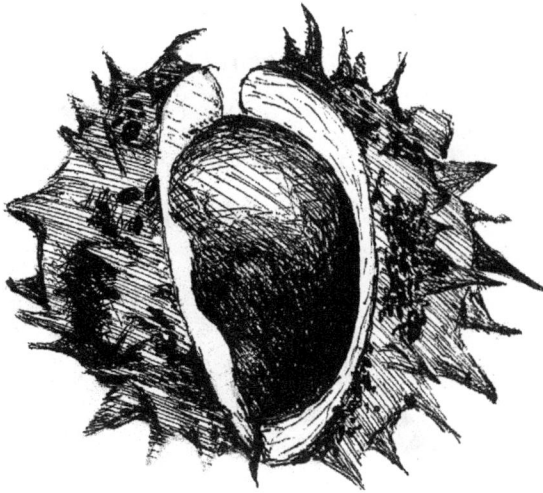

Bonfire

Mystic secrets in the whispers of trees,
Protected in embers with elegant ease.
Its blazing tongues
keep me at bay,
Though I desperately want to know what they say.
But its fiery wrath pushes me back
Squinting at the flickering words in black.
I watch as sparks dance out of sight,
To tell the tales of the trees
to the stars of the night.

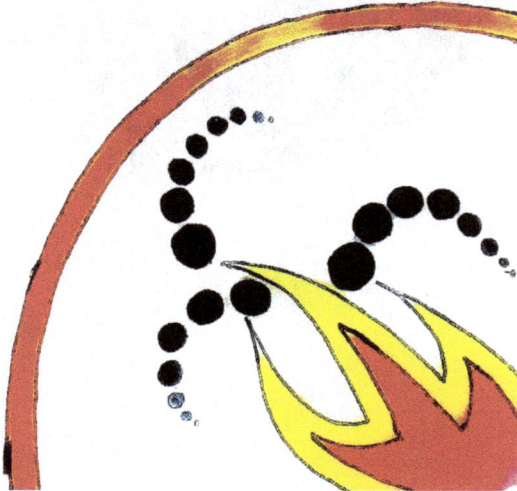

Scarecrow

Crucified bag of straw which everything ignores,
Arms stretched out in despair, not love
Or even threat; useless fingers flapping at the sky.
Perpetual is your plastic exclamation,
Indignant, as, more lively, predators
Take and dig and pick at the charge you guard.

Look both ways indeed but the wind speeds unseen,
Clattering across your bangles
And shoving your hair slantwise.
It drops out of the race of clouds
To baffle and bundle and bustle
Its transience around you: fixed.

To bend down and brush from your hem
The droplets of hose-water sprayed
By a careless gardener is beneath you,
His staunch lackey in his field,
More faithful than the sunshine,
The sunshine which spirals

Down your ringlet-orange curls
Into shadow then rain. It's the rain which laughs
The beige out of your tired overcoat.
No rest for the devoted.

Those two criss-cross saucer eyes reflect it all
As even in our English dilution of the summer sun
You cannot doze. You just stand and watch
But not scare the crows.

Screwball

Love is like one of those funny ice-creams.
Once the lid is peeled back, the awkward frost melts
And hot tongues curl around sweet hopes and dreams.

Warmed by the gentle sun of affection,
Soon we're sipping a sugar-smooth nectar,
Sharing the delights of this cool confection.

The cold is chilling the warmth inside
As the ball of gum at the bottom is reached.
Both cream and cup are gone now, set aside.

The gum's an undertaking of unknown duration.
At first, we chew with ardour, enjoying the taste,
But the taste soon fades and chewing means dedication.

Some cherish the Chew – it becomes second nature –
But we're getting nothing from this damp chicle

So we spit it out.

Changes

Gone is the world
Where even the simplest things are a work of art:
The elegant twist of a lamppost,
    The inlaid flourish of a wooden chair,
        That hail-fellow smile from the shop-keeper.
Now we live in a world of straight lines,
Sharp corners,
Monochrome surfaces,
And faces.

    With a punch,

The everyday poetry of furniture and style,
Which used to bring a smile to the face of fashion,
Devolved over mere decades,
And the world as it is came into being,
A world which doesn't have time or energy
For love or beauty.

Where is the humanity in Nouveau?

A time to be silent and a time to speak,

A time to love and a time to hate,

A time for war and a time for peace.

Cold Silence

Darkness echoes back at me
In harmony with the running water.
The silence listens.
It can't hear the written words.
They lie dead, echoless.
But I've read the prophecies
And profanities scratched into the same wall.
I found a truth hidden in the letters
Which the silence could not hear:
'Go to Hell, bastard.'
Weighed and found wanting.

Crack open the door,
Crack open the silence,
Crack open the darkness,
And let light stream in on cracked tiles.
I'll scrape the silence from these walls
And whitewash them with rhymes, notes, riffs
Which bounce along the bitter scrawl,
Those dead words.

But stubborn words still swear
And stubborn taps still splash,
Silence still can't hear
And stubborn tongues still lash.
So kick the door shut
And I'll return to the dripping, crying echoes
In this cold Silence.

Some hearts

Are an open book,

To be read and interpreted.

Language in a book changes views,

Transforms opinion.

So use words to polish hearts,

To clear the muddy waters.

Use words to mine the diamond from the rough.

To show true colours.

Iago's Guide

Do but see the vice of opinion
Where different eyes perceive
Words of a mask that others don
As the true or false they're meant to see.

General and maiden be lately wed
And in love so pure and heady t'is beyond chagrin.
Frame the lieutenant to disrupt their marital bed
And let the sly situational subversion begin.

First, set thy pestilence to the insecure ear
And leave the poison to work its way.
Feed the eyes with what they are told is there;
Let the green-eyed monster out to prey.

'Haply for she is white and he black –
Has she sealed up his eyes as close as oak?
Of conversation he has not the chamberer's knack...'
Just generally the embers of insecurity stoke.

It is decided in his tortured mind.
He vows his fairest warrior, a pitchy beast.
Have him leave all true love and duty behind
As you paint him as absent from her fruit-some feast.

All he wants now is ocular 'proof',
A thing to shew his marital strife,
To confirm in his mind thy twisted truth;
A thing easily got from your rattle-brained wife.

So take strawberries from the visage of Dian
And them bestow to one of another's bed.
Black vengeance in hollow cell liven
And watch those green eyes turn a choleric red.

Let him ask for himself the strawb'rries of Dian
(Trifles light as air jealousy turns to holy writ).
He still will see a monstrous horned man
So now you can pull and twist the ass's gag bit.

Have him go to her room once the servant's withdrawn
And inspire those fingers to turn rosy cheeks blue.
Her pale innocence comes on him, sudden as dawn.
Then watch as grief drives him to take his life too.

When your deeds be found out, they'll enquire of you why.
But refuse, let naught else ope thy lips.
For thy reasons leave erudite minds so belied,
You'll be ever etched on history's script.

*Inspired by Shakespeare's **Othello***

A time for nonsense!

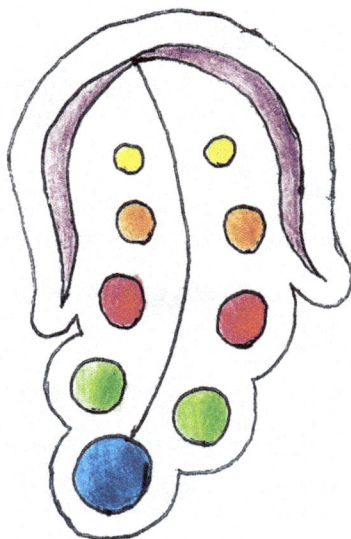

Tinfoil Pie

Line your dish with new tin foil,
Then heap in 2 spades of soil.
Fill the rest with starlit dreams
Of pots of gold and custard crèmes.
The ones that float around your head
Long after you have left your bed.

A colourful clown on a magic trapeze;
Your old dressing gown all smelling of cheese;
A battered bear you found in a bin;
The coin at the bottom of Gran's glass of gin;
Musical notes, a mystical sound;
A pixie caught when the moon was round.
They hide in forests of paper-leaved trees
And swim in the rainbow-coloured custard seas.

But make it only when the moon is full,
Or the foil and mud will make you ill.
With no moon it will taste like ashes and smoke;
When crescent it tastes like sad artichoke!

At the right time, it'll melt in your mouth:
Home-baked toothpaste and candyfloss trout.

But hurry, this pie can't be kept in a fridge.
You must eat it all up; every last smidge.
If left, the pie will most likely implode,
And suck in the windows and part of the road.

It's imploded; it's sucking us in.
What a horrible noise! Hope the neighbours aren't in.
Look, it's slowing; we won't die after all.
Clean up the kitchen, the toilet, the hall.
As for the road, you won't get very far,
If your vehicle is buried in 6 feet of tar!

In Vain

One summer day,
We had some warm rain.
I didn't want to get damp,
So when I saw a lit lamp,
I hurried on by
And met Madame Butterfly.

She was as pretty as can be
And seemed pleased to meet me.
She offered some honey-suckle tea.

I gently declined
Because I couldn't see why,
When I was standing right there,
She was addressing the mirror and doing her hair!

The sun came out
And away went the rain.
I promptly departed
And never visited again.

In God's time…

Black Angel

Running through the endless black,
Never turning or looking back.
But up ahead whats that I see?
A light,
A candle, it maybe.
Nearer, nearer,
Bigger, bigger.
I think, I think. . .
My Lord?

I cannot write a psalm

As King David did
And supplication's not my style.
Though I enjoy slotting words together
Into complex patterns and clever-dick meanings,
They never feel quite right.
Just shapes in my mouth,
They don't expand or transform
So how can I use them to pray?
My heart is an open book,
Written in emotion not words.
Proofread this, Abba,
Correct my spelling and grammar
Until the message is clear as the Lamb.

Great One

His hands cup the mountains,
His breath turning them golden.
His tears fall to the ground,
A musical sound;
And the streams echo His laughter.
Each little man,
The work of His hand.
Each animal a fine piece of art.
Stones sing His praise:
The world's swamped with His grace.

Candle

My words are so warm in my heart –
Warm and closer to You.
The world twists and distorts them;
Out there they have a job to do.

The candle I'm shielding warms my hands,
Glowing between my fingers mildly.
Should it really be leaping at the dark?
A fierce flame dancing at the cold winds wildly?

Those cold winds could blow it out;
Is that not the case with some?
But it's right that this warmth isn't mine to hoard,
There should be comfort for all who come.

www.ingramcontent.com/pod-product-compliance
Lightning Source LLC
Chambersburg PA
CBHW051047030426
42339CB00006B/238